Rainy Day
THINGS TO MAKE

Devised by Alison Boyle
Illustrated by Tessa Richardson-Jones

CONTENTS

2   Barmy boxes
4   Skyscraper skittles; Bookworm bookmark
6   Stained glass window
8   Munching caterpillar; Something afoot!
10   Jungle magic
12   An advent box; Let's fly a kite!
14   Prehistoric world
16   Funny faces; Paint on wax
18   Beside the seaside
20   Punch and Judy show
22   Plasticine printer; Happy Birthday surprise
24   Hissing Medusa
26   The weatherman; Hallowe'en shadows
28   Spider mobile
30   Home-made movie madness

Barmy boxes

You will need

a large piece of card
tracing paper
a ruler
scissors
glue
paints and paintbrush, or crayons
gummed paper (optional)
a ball-point pen which has run out
  of ink

Trace shapes 1 and 2 carefully. Check your measurements — all squares are 6cm×6cm, and all flaps are 1cm wide. Copy shapes 1 and 2 on to the card and colour them brightly. (See page 32 for instructions on how to copy a tracing.)

Cut around the edges and along the solid lines marked with an arrow.

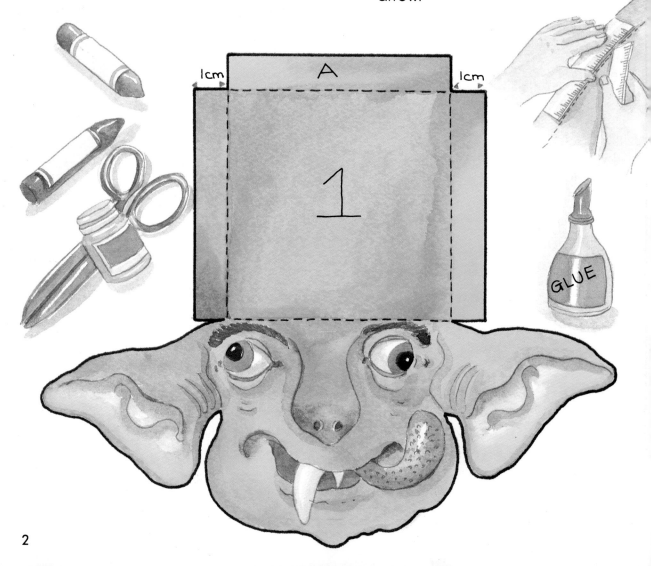

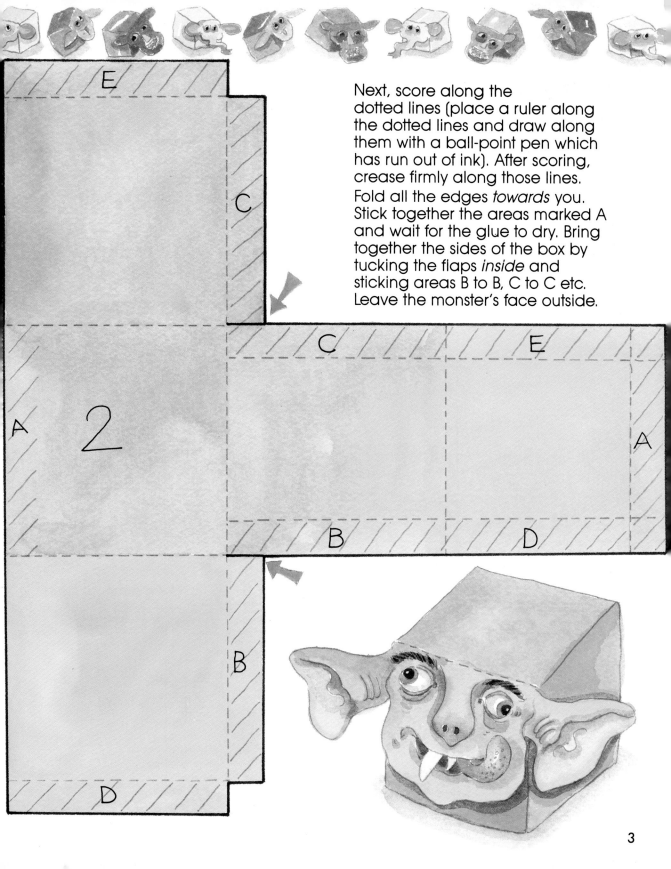

E

C

A

2

A

C

E

B

D

A

B

D

Next, score along the dotted lines (place a ruler along the dotted lines and draw along them with a ball-point pen which has run out of ink). After scoring, crease firmly along those lines.

Fold all the edges *towards* you. Stick together the areas marked A and wait for the glue to dry. Bring together the sides of the box by tucking the flaps *inside* and sticking areas B to B, C to C etc. Leave the monster's face outside.

Skyscraper skittles

You will need
a large piece of card
a ruler
scissors
paints and paintbrush or felt-tip pens
marbles

Measure, draw and cut out of the card two skyscraper shapes 10cm×15cm, two shapes 15cm×10cm, and two shapes 7cm×25cm, as shown.

Colour in the skyscrapers, adding windows and doors. Number them 2, 5 or 10, as shown. Cut a slit 1cm into the middle of the base of each piece.

Cut out six shapes 6cm×2cm, for stands. On each shape, make a slit half-way along the long edge, into the centre. Slot them into the cuts in the bases of the skyscrapers.

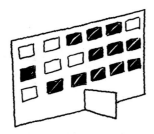

Position the skyscraper city on a smooth floor. Roll marbles to knock over the skittles. Play against yourself, trying to beat your best score, or play with friends. The winner is the one with the highest score after, say, six turns each.

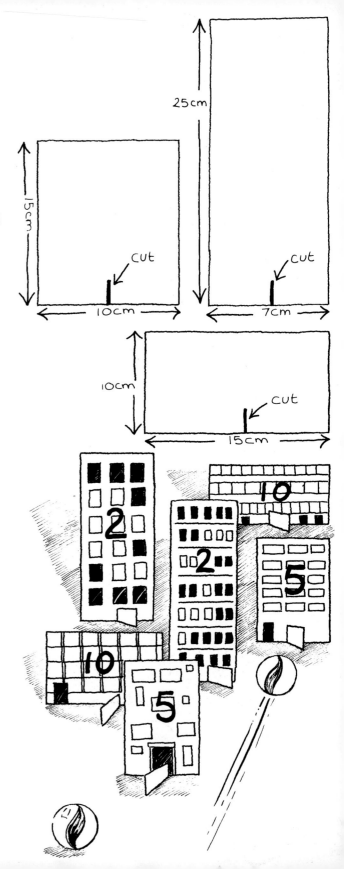

4

Bookworm bookmark

You will need
tracing paper
a piece of card
scissors
pale pink paint and paintbrush
a thick black felt-tip pen

Trace the worm shape then copy
it on to the card. (See page 32
for instructions on how to copy
a tracing.) Cut out the shape.

Using the pen, draw in the worm's
glasses, mouth, eyes, and the lines
across both sides of its body. Write
'This book belongs to' and add
your name.

Mix the paint and colour the front
of the worm's body — leave the
eyes white. Allow the paint to dry.
Now paint the other side of the
worm's body, but this time cover all
of the head area. Allow to dry.

Fold along the broken line, and
put the worm inside your book —
witn its head over the front.

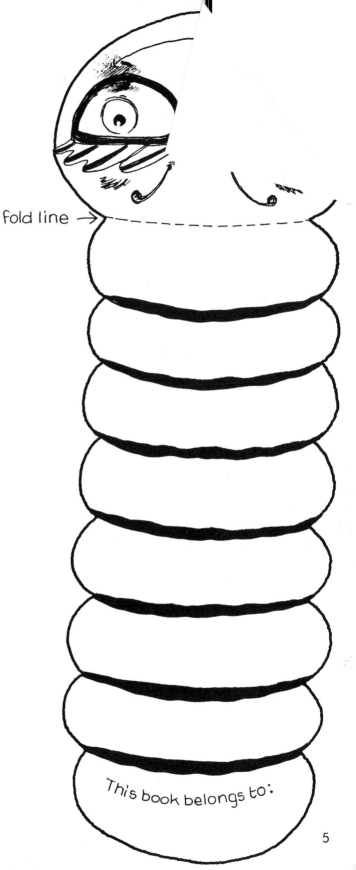

fold line →

This book belongs to:

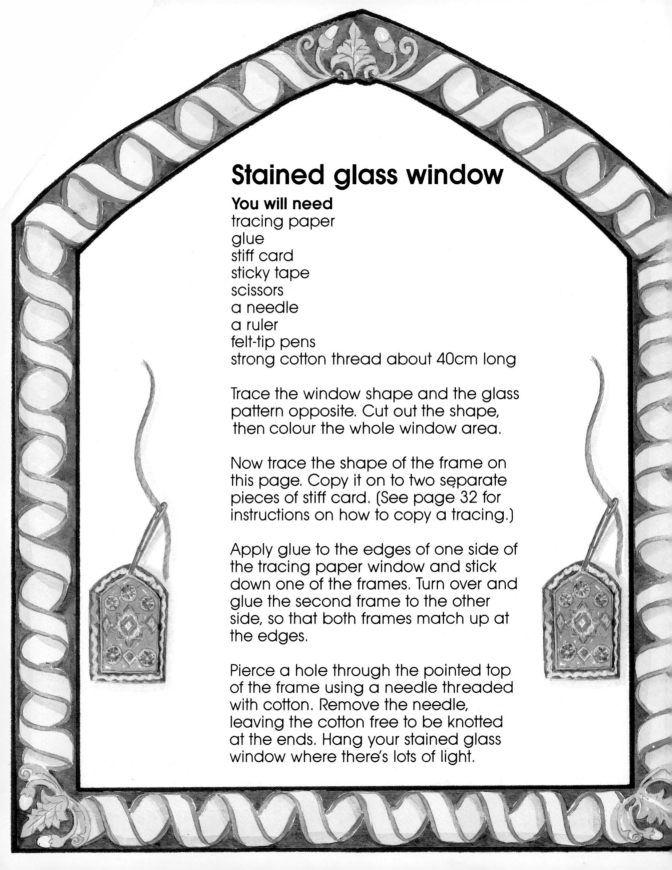

Stained glass window

You will need
tracing paper
glue
stiff card
sticky tape
scissors
a needle
a ruler
felt-tip pens
strong cotton thread about 40cm long

Trace the window shape and the glass pattern opposite. Cut out the shape, then colour the whole window area.

Now trace the shape of the frame on this page. Copy it on to two separate pieces of stiff card. (See page 32 for instructions on how to copy a tracing.)

Apply glue to the edges of one side of the tracing paper window and stick down one of the frames. Turn over and glue the second frame to the other side, so that both frames match up at the edges.

Pierce a hole through the pointed top of the frame using a needle threaded with cotton. Remove the needle, leaving the cotton free to be knotted at the ends. Hang your stained glass window where there's lots of light.

Munching caterpillar

You will need

a green-threaded cotton reel, or
   empty cotton reel painted green
a pencil with a sharp end
two pipe cleaners
thin card
tracing paper
sheets of white paper
scissors
glue
paint and paintbrush

Trace the leaf shape six times.
Trace the prickle shape thirteen
times, and the foot shape twenty-
six times. Now copy all the shapes
on to the paper. (See page 32
for instructions on how to copy a
tracing.) Colour in the shapes and
cut them out.

Now trace the caterpillar. Copy it
on to the card, then paint it. When
the paint has dried, cut along all
the solid black cut lines.

Glue the prickle tabs and position
them all along the *top* of the
caterpillar's body. Glue the feet
tabs to the *bottom* of its body, two
underneath each prickle.

Glue the ends of the leaves and

stick feet
underneath

wind them around the pipe
cleaners. Push the pipe cleaners
and pencil into the cotton reel
hole (the pencil point should stick
out, as shown). Place above a
radiator or near a warm air current.

Now balance the caterpillar on
the pencil (the dot in the centre
of the caterpillar should sit on the
point of the pencil). With a little
push, the caterpillar will spin.

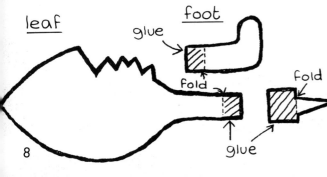

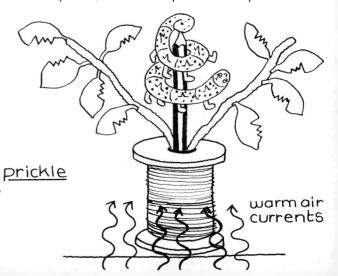

warm air
currents

8

hedgehog

shrew

squirrel

Something afoot!

You will need
a large piece of white card
peanut butter
fine peat or potting compost
water
a bowl
a spoon
string or ribbon
a hole punch or scissors

dormouse

Take the card, the bowl and a spoonful of peanut butter outside before you go to bed. Place the card in a sheltered spot, near some shrubs or a hedge. Place the peanut butter in the centre of the card, and put a ring of the peat mixture around it.

mouse

Hungry animals will have to step through the mixture to get to the food, and they should leave their footprints on the card.

Collect the card in the morning and match up the footprints with the shapes on this page.

Try the same thing a few days later, then weeks later. Are there more or

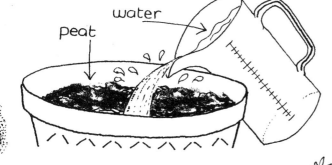

water

peat

My Nature Scrapbook

dog

Mix a few large spoonfuls of the peat or potting compost with water until the mixture is sloppy but not too runny.

less visitors? What are they? Keep an all-year-round record in a Nature Scrapbook.

cat

peanut butter

peat

Jungle magic

You will need

a polystyrene block about 3cm
  thick, 10cm long and 7cm wide
sheets of white paper
one very large sheet of paper
very thick card
tracing paper
poster paint
a thick paintbrush
an old baking tray
pins   scissors   glue
scrap paper
newspaper

Trace the elephant shape below.
Copy it on to the thick card and
cut out each piece. (See page 32
for instructions on how to copy a
tracing.)

Use the pins to attach the pieces
to the polystyrene
block.

Spread out plenty of newspaper
(save some for later).

Decide what colour to make your
elephant, and in the baking tray,
mix plenty of thick paint in this
colour.

Press the side of the polystyrene
block with the elephant pieces into
the paint. Make sure the pieces
are well-covered. Lift out the block
then press it, paint side down, on
to a piece of paper to make a print.

Always make several test prints on
scrap paper first, then do a final
print on good paper.

Move the elephant's trunk, and its
legs. Press the block into the paint
again and make a print. Carry on
moving the elephant's head, tail,

ears, trunk and legs, making prints in each new position so that the elephant looks as though it is moving. You can make the elephant walk the other way by removing the pins and turning over the pieces of card so that they face in the opposite direction.

Make up more printing blocks — e.g. a parakeet, tiger or monkey. Add these to your elephant pictures and make up a story to link the pictures together. Paint a coloured background on each print. Stick your paintings in order on to the large sheet of paper.

1. Today is bath day.

2. Slowly, slowly to my pool.

3. Tiger slinks in the bushes.

4. Parakeet squawks hello.

5. Monkey swings by.

6. Here at last! hot day!

7. Mmm. Cool.

8. Care to try some.

9. That's right. All join in.

10. Finished for today.

11. Time for home.

12. THE END.

An advent box

You will need
25 small matchboxes, all the same
  size
glue
a piece of card
coloured sticky paper or paints
scissors

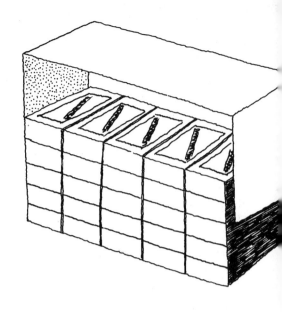

Glue the matchboxes on top of
each other in piles of five.

Stand the piles side by side and
glue them together to give you a
chest of twenty-five drawers.

Cut out a long strip of card so that
it fits right across the top of your
chest and down the sides.

Fold the strip of card carefully at
the corners, and glue it on to your
matchbox chest.

Paint the chest, and/or decorate
it with shapes cut from coloured
sticky paper.

Write the numbers 1–25 on the
fronts of the drawers, in any order
you choose.

Put a sweet or other small gift
(dice, rubber, marble, for example)
into each drawer and give the
advent box to a friend as an early
Christmas present.

6	12	14	9	16
10	24	3	4	1
15	2	21	5	19
11	18	25	17	22
7	13	20		23

Let's fly a kite!

You will need

a sheet of good quality writing
  paper, A4
a small, straight stick
a full reel of heavy-duty cotton
  thread
a stapler
sticky tape
a ruler
a pencil
coloured pencils, felt pens or
  paints
ribbon or bias binding
a safety pin

Colour or paint the paper on both
sides. (Draw your own design on it,
if you like.)

Fold the paper down the middle.

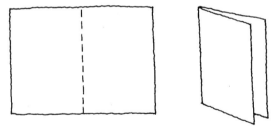

Mark a point 1cm in from the edge
at the top and bottom. Fold the
top flap along this line.

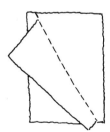

Fold the bottom flap in the same
way.

Put the kite flat on a table like this.
The wings of the kite should lie flat
on the table, and the folded part
— the keel — should stick up in the
air. Staple the keel together.

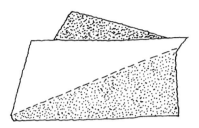

Turn the kite over and tape the
stick across the front. Tape the
two wings of the kite together.

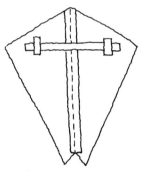

Make a few small holes with the
sharp point of a pencil in the keel.
You need to find out which hole
will allow your kite to fly best. Knot
your thread through each one in
turn and try out the kite when the
wind is reasonably strong and
steady. Pin on a long kite tail using
ribbon or bias binding.

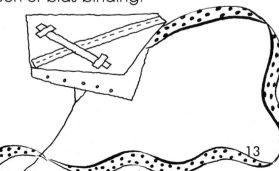

Prehistoric world

You will need

a large piece of stiff card (about 50cm x 50cm)
lots of old newspapers
wallpaper paste
a mixing tray
a thick brush
sheets of coloured paper (crepe paper can be used)
coloured paint
strong glue
sticky tape
a pencil
thick, coloured wool ⎫
pipe cleaners   ⎬ optional
felt   ⎪
false fur ⎭

Spread out layers of newspaper all over a big, clear area, and do all messy work on this.

Plan your landscape by labelling areas for mountains and rivers, forests and swamps on the card base.

Mix the paste in the tray and tear up small strips of the remaining newspaper. Dip each piece into the paste (use the brush to wipe off any extra paste) and lay it down on the stiff card.

Pile up the newspaper strips in mountain areas, and shape the mountains with your hands. Dig out caves by poking your finger into the side of a mountain!

Leave for 24 hours to dry thoroughly. When your landscape is dry, paint it — green for grassy areas, blue for rivers and so on.

To make the trees, roll sheets of green paper into tubes. Use sticky tape to hold the tubes in position. Make cuts at one end of each tube, from the edge to about half-way down. Gently push a pencil

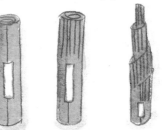

inside the tube from the other end. This pushes the inside of the tube upwards. To make branches, curl each cut strip, by pulling the strip along the edge of a ruler.

Use different heights of paper for variety, but make sure the paper is long enough to roll into a tube.

Make four small (1cm) upward cuts in the base of each tree, bend the paper outwards and glue the underneath of the paper to the baseboard. Hold in position until the glue is dry.

You can make big-leafed or brightly-coloured plants from pieces of felt and pipe cleaners.

Make animals out of newspaper and paste too. Make their feet large enough for them to balance, and their bodies the right size to fit into your landscape. Add bits of false fur. Paint the dinosaurs, and shape unusual humps with the newspaper strips. Use lots of wool for the Woolly Mammoth!

Funny faces

You will need
white, black and coloured paper
white scrap paper
a pencil
scissors
glue
scraps of wool, material, pipe
 cleaners, cotton wool, buttons
 etc.

Have a good look at your family,
friends, people in the street, your
pets, even yourself. On scrap
paper sketch out some of the
noses, chins, ear shapes, hair and
clothes that you see. Combine
some of these in one outline —
e.g. a crooked nose, big tummy,
big feet — on white paper.

Cut out this outline and stick it on
to black paper. Now add as many
bits from the scrap box as you
want, to 'dress' your caricature. Use
coloured paper too. Add props
and backgrounds.

Here is an example: a girl eating
a dripping ice-cream in the
sunshine. The girl has a long
tongue and a blobby nose. The
sun and its rays are made out of
felt. The ice-cream is made from

cotton wool, and the cone has
been specially drawn, cut out and
stuck down.

Paint on wax

You will need
a white candle
black poster paint
card
scissors
a paintbrush
a metal nail file or cocktail stick

Decide what size and shape of card to make, and cut it out. Mark the half-way point and cover the right-hand part with wax by rubbing a candle over the surface.

Use the point of the nail file or cocktail stick to scrape a design into the paint. The white wax will begin to show through the lines of your design.

Now cover this surface with four thick layers of black paint. Let each layer dry before you apply the next one.

Fold the card. Write your message inside. Copy these designs, or make up your own.

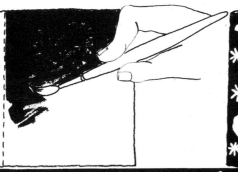

Beside the seaside

Have a peep at what it was like at the seaside in the 1920s!

You will need
a shoe box with a lid
two small boxes (single soap boxes
  are ideal)
thin card
poster paints
coloured tissue paper (light blue,
  dark blue, orange and red)
gummed paper (variety of colours)
a needle and thread
big safety pins
a ruler   scissors   glue

Make a small peephole in the middle of one of the shorter ends of the big box by pushing the point of the scissors through it (rest the end of the box on a firm base).

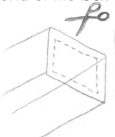

Measure the size of the shorter end and cut out this shape from light-blue tissue paper. At the opposite end to the hole, cut out a section from the box — leaving a frame around the edge. Cut a circle from the orange tissue paper for the sun, and a wave pattern out of dark-blue tissue paper. Glue these pieces on to the light-blue. Now stick this inside the frame.

Cut a panel out of the box lid, and stick red tissue paper over it.

Use a soap box for the Punch and Judy booth. Stand the box on end, and cut a rectangular shape out of the top half of the box front,

leaving a frame along the top and sides. Decorate the outside with strips of different-coloured gummed paper. Draw and colour puppets, cut them out and glue them to the inside of the box, so that they can be seen through the hole.

The other soap box can be the changing tent. Cut a door-shaped flap at the front and paint a surprised man or woman on the inside of the door. Push a threaded needle (knotted at the end) through the corner of the door, then through a suitable point on the box lid. Leave about 20cm of thread — attach this to a safety pin. Once the lid is on, you will be able to open and close the door by pulling the thread.

Paint the inside and outside of the big box and lid in appropriate colours. Add strips of yellow gummed paper around the peephole, to give the sun rays.

Draw, colour and cut out as many extras as you like. Put people on stands by slitting the bottom of the figure and pushing in a rectangle of card. Stick a long strip of card to other people's backs. Add two or three people to a long strip of card that is 15cm wider than the box. Make a hole in each side of the box and push the strip through. Stick card tabs to the ends of the strip, and move it from side to side.

Add seagulls and fish. Put on the box lid. Look through the peephole, pull the threads and the card strips.

Stand

Punch and Judy Show

You will need

an empty soap box (size E10 is
  ideal)
card
glue
tracing paper
wrapping paper — one sheet
  plain, one sheet striped
lollipop sticks
scissors
a ruler
felt-tip pens or paint

Mark the half-way point on each
of the longest edges on the front
of the box, and join them with a
horizontal line. On the *top* half of
the front, measure and draw a line
2cm in from the top, sides, and
half-way line. Cut out the area
within these lines.

Mark out and cut away a similar
shape on the back of the box, but
this time from the *bottom* half. You
will use this to move your puppets
around during the show.

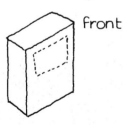

Use the card from the two cut-out
sections to decorate the top of the
box front. Cut out a border in two
pieces (the cut-out sections are

smaller than the width of the front),
paint them, then glue them on.

Glue strips of wrapping paper over
the box. Use stripy paper (stripes
going from top to bottom) for the
front.

Trace the puppet outlines. Copy
them on to the card and cut them

out. (See page 32 for instructions on how to copy a tracing.) Colour them brightly, then glue a lollipop stick to each puppet's back.

glue

Stand your theatre on a flat surface, with the back of the theatre towards you. Holding the puppets by the base of their lollipop sticks, and so that their backs are towards you, push them up through the hole in the back of the theatre, until they can be seen through the hole in the front. Write a script and invite your family to a show!

Plasticine® printer

You will need
a cotton reel
two pencils
glue
Plasticine®
a glass jar or bottle
poster paint
a tray
sheets of paper or card

Press the Plasticine® gently on to the reel.

Using the other pencil, design a pattern in the surface of the Plasticine® by pressing the pencil point into the Plasticine®.

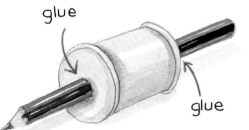

glue

glue

Push the pencil through the holes of the cotton reel, lightly gluing around each hole. Leave for ten minutes to harden.

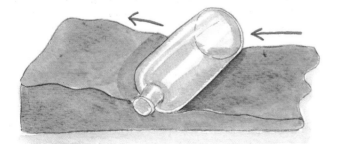

Using the jar as a rolling pin, roll a length of Plasticine® until it's about 1cm thick, and long enough to wrap around the reel.

Mix some poster paint with water in the tray. Roll the printer in the paint and push it across the paper or card to make a pattern. Print in different directions, cover some areas twice, or use only part of the roller, tilted. Add more colours letting each layer dry before you add another one. Wash the roller between colour changes.

Happy Birthday surprise

You will need
card
a ruler
scissors
glue
felt-tip pens

Cut out two pieces of card 15cm×15cm. Measure in 2cm from the edges of one piece of card and draw an inner square. Cut away this inner square, leaving a frame. On the other piece, leaving a 3cm border all around the edge, design and colour a wonderful birthday cake. Leave room for the name.

Glue the *outer edges* of the frame to the picture, at the *top* and *bottom* only, leaving the sides free.

Cut two pieces of card 12cm×7.5cm. Now cut out two tabs from the card. Glue the

straight edge of each tab to the middle of the longest edge of the two pieces of card.

Slot these two pieces of card *in between* the frame and the picture, so that the cake can't be seen any more.

Colour a bold parcel design over the whole surface, then pull the tabs at the side . . . surprise, surprise!

23

Hissing Medusa

Medusa was a mythical creature who had snakes for hair! Wear this snake mask for a fancy dress party, or give a friend a fright!

You will need
stiff card (enough for the mask)
white paper
tracing paper
30cm narrow elastic
glue
sticky tape
bright felt-tip pens (don't use paint, it might peel)
a ruler
scissors

B,C and D

Trace the mask outline, including all the boxes marked A, B, C, D, and features. Copy this on to the stiff card. (See page 32 for instructions on how to copy a tracing.) Cut out the eyes, mouth and nose holes (match them up to your face first, to check they're in the right position).

Trace the snake designs. Copy them on to the white paper. You need twenty large snakes and three small snakes. Design and colour amazing patterns on *each* side of the snakes' bodies.

Curl all the snakes by carefully running the edge of the ruler over the surface of the paper. Stick the large snakes by their tails to the positions marked A, and stick two of the small snakes by tail *and* tongue to positions B and C. Then stick the last small snake by its *tail* to D.

Push a pencil point carefully through the holes at each side of the mask. Thread the elastic through to fit.

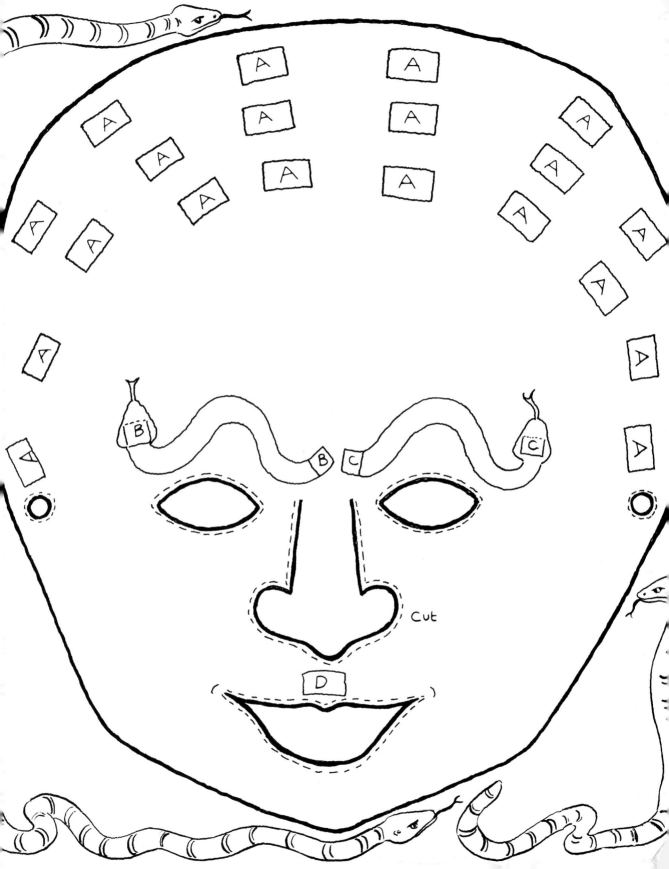

The weatherman

You will need
a large pine cone
two pipe cleaners
Plasticine®
a piece of scrap material
cotton wool
thread
felt pens
strands of wool
glue
paper
scissors

Turn the cone upside-down. Twist a pipe cleaner round the thick end, to look like arms.

Twist the other pipe cleaner round the bottom of the cone. Bend the two ends down to look like legs.

Add little Plasticine® feet.

Cut a circle out of the scrap of material. Shape it into a ball to make the head and stuff it with cotton wool. Tie it tightly with a piece of strong thread.

Draw a face on the head.

Glue strands of wool into place for hair.

Glue the head to the body.

Cut a paper collar and glue it into place to cover the join.

When the weather is dry, your weatherman's pine cone body will open up. When it is wet, the pine cone will stay closed.

Hallowe'en shadows

You will need
a large piece of white paper
a thick paintbrush
paints (lots of black)
a black felt-tip pen
stiff card ⎫
scissors ⎪
glue ⎬ (for the frame)
sticky tape ⎭

Using very small amounts of pink, blue and purple paints, mix each with plenty of water and brush them one by one over the whole area of the paper, using the thick brush. Try to create atmosphere with swishes and swirls. Leave the paper until it is properly dry.

Using the black pen, draw a bold, clear outline of your Hallowe'en

picture, making as many varied shapes as you can. Add bats and scary little creatures.

Outline too the spaces between the trees or branches and any other areas where you want the light-coloured wash to shine through. Use the black paint to colour in your picture, making sure you don't fill in the spaces you want to remain light.

Make a card frame very slightly smaller than the size of your painting by cutting away the centre of a piece of card. Stick the picture to the frame by taping along all the edges on the back. Make fancy corners from separate pieces of card stuck on with glue.

Spider mobile

You will need
strong card (not too thick)
paper or thin card
tracing paper
scissors
a needle
20cm strong cotton thread
ordinary cotton thread
paint/glitter paint/crayons

Trace the shape of the spider's
web, then copy it on to the thicker
card. (See page 32 for instructions

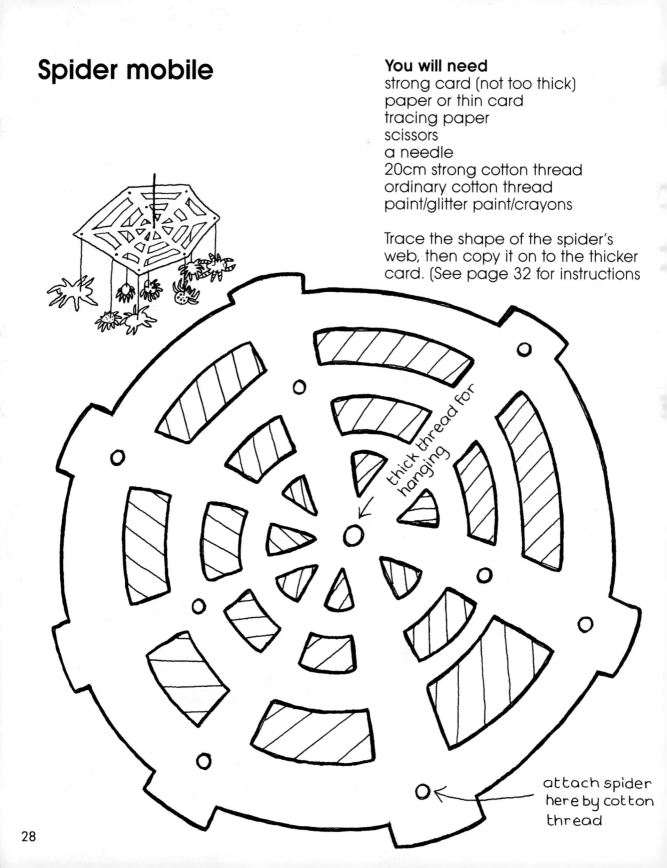

thick thread for
hanging

attach spider
here by cotton
thread

28

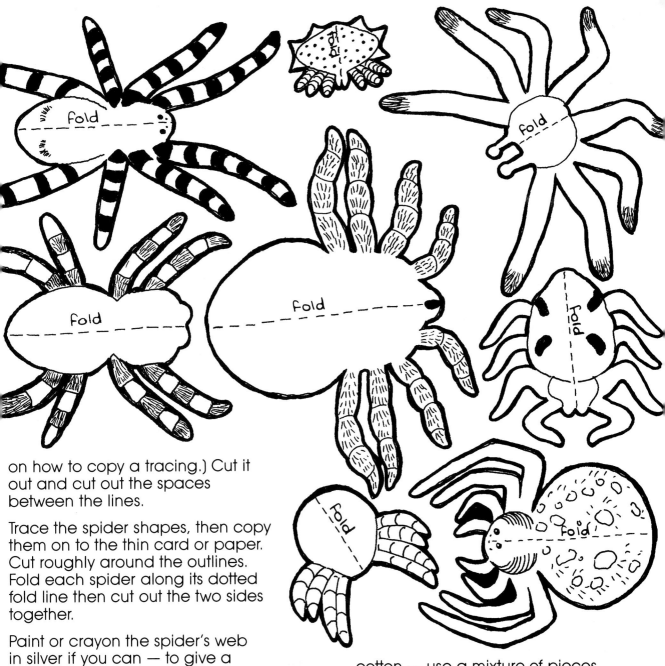

on how to copy a tracing.) Cut it out and cut out the spaces between the lines.

Trace the spider shapes, then copy them on to the thin card or paper. Cut roughly around the outlines. Fold each spider along its dotted fold line then cut out the two sides together.

Paint or crayon the spider's web in silver if you can — to give a shimmery effect like a real web. Colour and decorate all the spiders .

Thread one length of cotton (doubled up and knotted at one end) at a time into a needle and through the centre of a spider's fold-line. Vary the lengths of your

cotton — use a mixture of pieces between 10cm and 30cm. Then push the needle through one of the points marked on the web, knotting the doubled end to secure it. When all the spiders are attached, use the strong thread to tie up the web. Thread it in the same way, doubled and knotted.

29

Home-made movie madness

Make up a film library — from loony cartoons to nature documentaries.

glue

glue

hold with ribbon or glue

You will need

a shoe box
two long pencils or pieces of
  wooden dowel long enough to
  stretch across the width of the box
long strips of paper
newspapers, magazines and
  comics
scissors
sticky tape
glue
felt-tip pens or paints
gummed paper or scrap material

Decorate around your screen with pieces of scrap material or coloured gummed paper to create a curtain effect.

If your shoe box is the type which does not have a lid, you must cut a hole in the back (the side opposite the screen) large enough for you to get your hand inside easily. If your box does have a lid, just leave the lid off — you don't need it.

Decide what your film is to be about, then either draw your own pictures or cut them out of magazines. You could cut out the

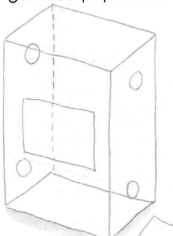

Cut a screen out of one long side of the box. (The size depends on the size of film you want to make.) About 5cm from the top and bottom of each of the shorter side sections, pierce holes, using a pencil. Stand the box on end.

funniest images from cartoon strips in newspapers or comics, and stick a number of them together to make a 'Continuing Adventures Of The Great . . .'

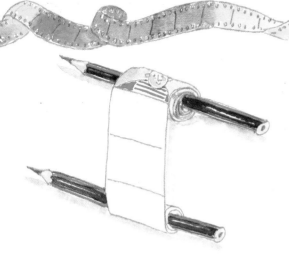

Your pictures should be glued in sequence on to a strip of paper to make a long reel of 'film'. (You may need to glue shorter strips together to make a long strip.) Leave at least 6cm blank at each end of the strip. Make sure that the size of your film matches the size of your screen.

Attach a pencil to each end of the reel using sticky tape. Roll most of the reel on to the top pencil, stopping when the first picture is just visible.

Put the film reel into the cinema screen through the back opening and, from inside, slot first the bottom then the top pencil through the holes at the side of the box.

Roll the film from the full pencil to the empty one.

If you make a number of films, it is best to attach each film to separate pencils, so that you can do a quick changeover.

Instead of using ready-made cartoons, you could try adding your own speech bubbles (cut out of white paper) to ordinary pictures!

If you draw and colour your own film, it could be about a spooky castle with purple and green backgrounds, a black and white movie, or a true life story about your family, friends or pets. If you want to make films in a larger size, just use another box and change the size of the viewing hole.

Invite a few friends to a private viewing of your films! Try to have a well-rehearsed commentary. Mimic the voices of the famous cartoon characters, make spooky screams and gurgles for the fantasy films, and speak clearly for your documentaries.

This edition published by Limited Editions in 1996

First published by Arrow Books Ltd
62-5 Chandos Place, London WC2N 4NW

An imprint of Century Hutchinson Ltd

London   Melbourne   Sydney   Auckland
Johannesburg and agencies throughout the world

First published 1988

Set in 12/13 point Avantgarde Book by
Quadraset Ltd, Midsomer Norton
Produced by Oyster Books Ltd, Weare, Somerset
Printed in China

ISBN 0 09 956160 3

Making and copying a tracing

1   Lay the tracing paper over the picture you want to trace.

2   Using a pencil, trace firmly over all the lines of the picture. Then lift the tracing paper off the picture.

3   *Turn the tracing over.* On this reverse side, using a soft pencil, shade over all the lines you have just drawn.

4   Now turn your tracing the right way up again. Lay it on top of the piece of paper or card you want to copy the tracing on to.

5   Holding the tracing steady, use your pencil to go over all the lines of the picture. The pencil shading on the reverse allows the lines of the tracing to be transferred on to the paper or card.

6   Lift off the tracing. Go over any lines which have not come out clearly on the paper or card. Your tracing is now complete.